THE PERFECT
YOU
·WORKBOOK·

F

D0390709

THE PERFECT YOU

· WORKBOOK ·

A BLUEPRINT FOR IDENTITY

DR. CAROLINE LEAF

BakerBooks

a division of Baker Publishing Group
Grand Rapids, Michigan

© 2018 by Caroline Leaf

Published by Baker Books
a division of Baker Publishing Group
PO Box 6287, Grand Rapids, MI 49516-6287
www.bakerbooks.com

Printed in the United States of America

All rights reserved. No part of this publication may be reproduced, stored in a retrieval system, or transmitted in any form or by any means—for example, electronic, photocopy, recording—without the prior written permission of the publisher. The only exception is brief quotations in printed reviews.

ISBN: 978-0-8010-7797-5

Unless otherwise indicated, Scripture quotations are from the New King James Version®. Copyright © 1982 by Thomas Nelson, Inc. Used by permission. All rights reserved.

Scripture quotations labeled AMP are from the Amplified® Bible, copyright © 2015 by The Lockman Foundation. Used by permission. (www.Lockman.org)

Scripture quotations labeled ESV are from The Holy Bible, English Standard Version® (ESV®), copyright © 2001 by Crossway, a publishing ministry of Good News Publishers. Used by permission. All rights reserved. ESV Text Edition: 2011

Scripture quotations labeled NIV are from the Holy Bible, New International Version®. NIV®. Copyright © 1973, 1978, 1984, 2011 by Biblica, Inc.™ Used by permission of Zondervan. All rights reserved worldwide. www.zondervan.com

Scripture quotations labeled NLT are from the Holy Bible, New Living Translation, copyright © 1996, 2004, 2015 by Tyndale House Foundation. Used by permission of Tyndale House Publishers, Inc., Carol Stream, Illinois 60188. All rights reserved.

Portions of this text have been taken from The Perfect You, published by Baker Books, 2017.

This publication is intended to provide helpful and informative material on the subjects addressed. Readers should consult their personal health professionals before adopting any of the suggestions in this book or drawing inferences from it. The author and publisher expressly disclaim responsibility for any adverse effects arising from the use or application of the information contained in this book.

19 20 21 22 23 24   7 6 5 4 3

In keeping with biblical principles of creation stewardship, Baker Publishing Group advocates the responsible use of our natural resources. As a member of the Green Press Initiative, our company uses recycled paper when possible. The text paper of this book is composed in part of post-consumer waste.

Contents

Introduction   7

How to Use This Workbook   11

Prologue   13

1 The Big Picture   23

2 The Perfect You: *Thinking, Feeling, Choosing*   34

3 Discovering the Potential of Our Blueprint
for Identity   41

4 The Philosophy of the Perfect You   52

5 The Science of the Perfect You   67

6 AND 7 Profiling the Perfect You: *The Unique Qualitative (UQ)
Assessment Tool* / The Perfect You Checklist   83

8 The Discomfort Zones   86

9 AND 10 The Perfect You Chart / Perfect You Metacognitive
Module Exercises   91

Conclusion   93

The Perfect You Reading List   95

Introduction

See the Read-along Instructions on the DVD.

Who am I?

We all, at one point in our lives, ask ourselves this question. We are who we are, but unveiling our identity and activating it correctly are crucial to a life well-lived; this question is the theme of countless books, both classic and modern, fiction and nonfiction. It shapes some of the greatest masterpieces in the world of art and characterizes the world of education. It is a question that none of us can escape—a question that can only be measured by the individual as an individual: *Can I accept the way God has allowed me to be?*

In *The Perfect You*, I discussed this question of identity and how each of us has a unique way of thinking, feeling, and choosing. No two minds are alike—our ability to think, choose, and feel is our particular blueprint for identity.

I created this workbook to help you mindfully and intentionally self-evaluate in order to think deeply and understand and apply the

7

blueprint for identity in *The Perfect You*. Each key section and statement follows the chapters of *The Perfect You* book, with a series of challenging questions that will help you understand the Perfect You as well as the purpose of the powerful **Unique Qualitative (UQ) Assessment Tool**. You will find that these questions will show you how the UQ tool is an organic process that takes place as you discover your blueprint for identity. The UQ assessment is in *The Perfect You*, on pages 109–234, not in this workbook.

As you work sequentially through the workbook, you will find the answers to the questions are all in *The Perfect You*, so you will need to have it with you at all times as you work through this workbook.

It is very important that you find and answer the questions of this workbook from your Perfect You perspective—make that brain work! Think deeply. Think of as many examples as you can in your own life—that is, what you are thinking, feeling, choosing, and doing. Evaluate them and write down your thoughts as you progress through the book and workbook. Try to avoid common, rote phrases and "Christianese" in your answers.

Once you have completed the questions in each chapter, there is a discussion section that draws on Scripture to help you see the connection between science and the Bible. I would recommend working through the questions and Scripture discussions a second time, after you have completed the workbook and filled in the UQ assessment, which will help you apply the principles discussed in *The Perfect You*. In fact, you can continually reuse this workbook, because each time you go through it you will discover more about yourself and how you function moment by moment in your life. You will come to a deeper understanding of how to see your experiences as an encounter with the infinite beauty of God—as a journey into the reflection of your part in him.

Chapters 6, 7, 9, and 10 of the book do not have corresponding study chapters in this workbook, since they cover the UQ profile and Perfect You checklist, which you will need to work through in the actual *The Perfect You* book. However, there is a simple introduction into the purpose and use of these chapters.

I have used multiple translations of the Bible throughout this guide. If you wish to use a different translation, translate the Scripture yourself, or use multiple translations of the same verses, you are more than welcome to! Shifting between translations forces you to analyze the Scripture from a variety of different viewpoints, which increases mind health.

How to Use This Workbook

1. Get a blank notebook in which you will write your answers to the questions.

2. Follow the chapters in the book *The Perfect You*. Have *The Perfect You* open alongside the workbook as you watch the DVD.

3. Each of the numbered items in each workbook chapter focuses on a key idea from the DVD. That key idea is in italics, and it's also highlighted in the DVD slides. The book, too, features these ideas. These are the big ideas you need to absorb as you go along.

4. Pause the DVD after each numbered item is covered. Read the relevant paragraphs in *The Perfect You*. In your notebook, write your answers to the questions under that numbered item. Think deeply and write as fully as you can. If you are meeting with a group, take as much time as you need to discuss the questions. Then start the DVD again. Don't be in a hurry to cover all of the questions of a chapter in one group meeting.

5. After you finish the DVD segment for a chapter, turn to the Bible passages provided in this workbook. Think about how they reflect or respond to the ideas discussed in the DVD. Write your thoughts in your notebook or discuss them with your group.

Let's begin!

Prologue

See pages 16–19 in *The Perfect You*.

As we begin this journey, it's vitally important to bear two points in mind. First, intense mental effort changes brain patterns. Second, your intentional and powerful thoughts change your brain, so make sure they are God's thoughts!

1. *Who am I? Does anyone out there understand me? Am I merely the product of blind evolutionary forces or what Richard Dawkins calls a "stroke of dumb luck" in a material world? Or do I have purpose and meaning, a unique part in a divine plan? Does anyone understand who I am, or who I am meant to be? Do I even understand me? Can I accept the way God has allowed me to be? Do I really accept the blueprint for identity that God has given me?* Before you look at any other questions, write your answers to these questions in your notebook and then see how they change as you work through the book, workbook, and DVD.

_____

_____

_____

_____

_____

_____

_____

2. *God does understand you. He placed significance in you—your "Perfect You."* What is the Perfect You? How do you understand the Perfect You in terms of being an image-bearer of God? What do you think "blueprint for identity" means? How does the Perfect You relate to your particular blueprint for identity?

_____

_____

_____

_____

_____

_____

_____

_____

_____

_____

_____

3. *You create your unique reality and shape your brain with your thoughts.* Even though you haven't worked through the profile yet, after reading the second paragraph in the book's prologue, what do you hope to learn from the Unique Qualitative (UQ) Assessment Tool? Why is it unique? How do you think it will help you understand your Perfect You? You can look back at these answers when you have worked through the chapters leading up to the profile and after you have filled in your profile—I believe it will be enlightening. Remember to try not to use standard "Christianese" or "I am gifted" phrases in your answers. I want you to think deeply about your encounter with a loving, personal God who gives you identity and to use the scientific principles I discuss to explore this idea. Start developing a new vocabulary about what a blueprint for identity really is.

_____

_____

_____

_____

_____

_____

_____

_____

_____

_____

_____

_____

_____

_____

4. *Development and growth are organic and ongoing.* What do "development" and "growth" mean in terms of the Perfect You? Is growth immediate? Or is it a long-term process? Will you ever stop growing or learning how to be who you were created to be? If this is a long-term process, what are the implications of this for you as a human being?

_____

_____

_____

_____

_____

5. *You can't live in your purpose if you don't identify your blueprint and operate in your Perfect You.* How do you understand the relationship between identity, purpose, and reflecting God's glorious image to the world? Have you ever been in a situation where you felt as if you did not know who you were? How did this feeling affect your ability to live your life and do what you love to do? How did it affect your motivation? Did you, or do you, feel inner conflict as you were, or are, trying to be someone you are not? And how did this sense of "being lost" impact your relationship both with God and with other people? What "locks up" your Perfect You?

_____

_____

_____

_____

_____

6. *We have to see God's image reflected in us if we truly want to understand our unique blueprint for identity.* How do you understand the "image of God"? How does it relate to your identity? What does your identity have to do with love? Is this something everyone is looking for? Can we be truly "happy" if we don't understand who we are?

_____

_____

_____

_____

_____

_____

7. *Although you may not think you do, you actually know who you are!* Is there any connection between the way you think, speak, and act and your Perfect You—do you have Perfect You moments when you think, speak, and act? Do you feel like you have a particular way of thinking, speaking, and acting? How so? Do you notice that the people you know also have unique ways of thinking, speaking, and acting? Do you tolerate and try to understand their differences? Or do these differences frustrate you? Think of an example in your own life.

_____

_____

_____

_____

_____

_____

8. *Yet you are not defined by where you are or where you have been, but where you will be. Finding out who you are at your very core is a journey, and it can be an awe-inspiring one, depending on the attitude you adopt!* How do you understand "attitude"? Do you think you can choose your attitude, or, rather, choose how you react to life? Do you feel as if your past defines who you are and determines your present attitude? Does this affect your sense of identity? How does this affect your ability to make wise decisions?

_____

_____

_____

_____

_____

9. *The more you unlock your Perfect You, the more miracles you will activate in your life and the lives of the people around you.* What is the relationship between knowing who you are and serving and loving others? How is this connected to being an image-bearer of God?

_____

_____

_____

_____

_____

10. *The more you step into your Perfect You, the more intelligent you will become; the more gifts, skills, and abilities you will develop; the more your relationships will improve; the more your mental health will improve; the more your physical health will improve; the more joy you will find; the more you will see others through the eyes of God; the more humble you will become, because you will see his magnificence in you; the more you will understand yourself and others; the more you will desire to help others; and the more you will celebrate others instead of envying them.* What is the connection between all these and the Perfect You? How does this help you serve and love other people? Is there a relationship between stewardship, service, humility, and identity? How so? Do you want this to happen in your life? Why?

DISCUSSION

In light of the information in this chapter, focusing on the hope that science gives us alongside Scripture, discuss the following verses:

1. **Jeremiah 1:5 (AMP):** "Before I formed you in the womb I knew you [and approved of you as My chosen instrument], and before you were born I consecrated you [to Myself as My own]; I have appointed you as a prophet to the nations."

2. **Genesis 1:27 (NIV):** "So God created mankind in his own image, in the image of God he created them; male and female he created them."

3. **Matthew 4:18–22 (ESV):** "While walking by the Sea of Galilee, he saw two brothers, Simon (who is called Peter) and Andrew his brother, casting a net into the sea, for they were fishermen. And he said to them, 'Follow me, and I will make you fishers of men.' Immediately they left their nets and followed him. And going on from there he saw two other brothers, James the son of Zebedee and John his brother, in the boat with Zebedee their father, mending their nets, and he called them. Immediately they left the boat and their father and followed him."

4. **Ecclesiastes 3:11 (NIV):** "He has made everything beautiful in its time. He has also set eternity in the human heart; yet no one can fathom what God has done from beginning to end."

5. **Matthew 25:14–30 (ESV):** "For it will be like a man going on a journey, who called his servants and entrusted to them his property. To one he gave five talents, to another two, to another one, to each according to his ability. Then he went away. He who had received the five talents went at once and traded with them, and he made five talents more. So also he who had the two talents made two talents more. But he who had received the one talent went and dug in the ground and hid his master's money. Now after a long time the master of those servants came and settled accounts with them. And he who had received the five talents came forward, bringing five talents more, saying, 'Master, you delivered to me five talents; here, I have made five talents more.' His master said to him, 'Well done, good and faithful servant. You have been faithful over a little; I will set you over much. Enter into the joy of your master.' And he also who had the two talents came forward, saying, 'Master, you delivered to me two talents; here, I have made two talents more.' His master said to him, 'Well done, good and faithful servant. You have been faithful over a little; I will set you over much. Enter into the joy of your master.' He also who had received the one talent came forward, saying, 'Master, I knew you to be a hard man, reaping where you did not sow, and gathering where you scattered no seed, so I was afraid, and I went and hid your talent in the ground. Here, you have what is yours.' But his master answered him, 'You wicked and slothful servant! You knew that I reap where I have not sown and gather where I scattered no seed? Then you ought to have invested my money with the bankers, and at my coming I should have received what was my own with interest. So take the talent from him and give it to him who has the ten talents. For to everyone who has will more be given, and he will have an abundance. But from the one who has not, even what he has will be taken away. And cast the

worthless servant into the outer darkness. In that place there will be weeping and gnashing of teeth.'"

Write your conclusions from the discussion of these Scriptures linked to the ten points above:

1

The Big Picture

See pages 23–39 in *The Perfect You.*

1. *Our individual, unique responses are inspired and driven by our individual, unique design.* How does uniqueness relate to consciousness? What is a quale? Can you think of a particular situation where you and someone you know experienced the same event but perceived it differently?

_____

_____

_____

_____

_____

_____

_____

2. *If healthy, conscious experience is what it feels like to be in the Perfect You, then "what it feels like" for you means the specific set of associations you have previously made through the filter of your Perfect You.* What is meant by a "filter"? How does it affect the way you see the world? What thoughts and memories make up your filter? Give some examples. How are you "wired"?

_____

_____

_____

_____

_____

_____

3. *When we step out of our Perfect You, we will be in conflict and this will make us frustrated and unhappy, and even reduce our intelligence and potentially lead to mental ill health.* Why do you think you feel this way when you step out of your Perfect You? Have you experienced this frustration in your life; that is, have you ever felt like you were not thinking, speaking, or acting like yourself?

_____

_____

_____

_____

_____

4. *When we learn to focus on our God, who is love, and what he says about us, we learn how to embrace our unique identity and discover who we truly are in him.* What is the relationship between love and the Perfect You? How does this relate to what the Bible says about God and love?

_____

_____

_____

_____

_____

_____

5. *The Geodesic Information Processing Model conceptualizes how we uniquely think, feel, and choose, through the filter of our Perfect You, and the causal effect this has on our brains and thus our behavior.* What is this model? How is it connected to the Perfect You? What do you think the significance of the word *geodesic* (meaning global) is for you personally? Do you think you could have a transgenerational, global impact? What does this look like for you?

_____

_____

_____

_____

_____

_____

6. *Our thinking changes the structure of our brain because our mind is separate from our brain: this is called psycho-physical functioning.* How do you understand the mind and the brain? Are both physical organs? Is this what you learned in school or college? What is the relationship between the mind, the soul, and consciousness? How does this view relate to the Bible's teachings on the mind/soul/consciousness?

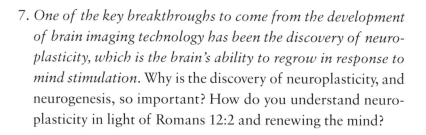

7. *One of the key breakthroughs to come from the development of brain imaging technology has been the discovery of neuroplasticity, which is the brain's ability to regrow in response to mind stimulation.* Why is the discovery of neuroplasticity, and neurogenesis, so important? How do you understand neuroplasticity in light of Romans 12:2 and renewing the mind?

8. *We are not merely the firing of our neurons on a colorful brain scan. There is a danger in seeing brain scans as a reliable and detailed road map to human consciousness.* Why is it important not to rely solely on brain scans in science? What is neuroreductionism?

_____

_____

_____

_____

_____

_____

9. *The universe is inherently interconnected—from the macro level to the subatomic level to the level of waves of energy; this is evident throughout the natural world.* Can we see this interconnectedness in Scripture? Think of the psalms.

_____

_____

_____

_____

_____

_____

10. *The moment when people recognize the power of their minds, the individuality of their thinking, and how they have control over their lives, they are truly able to transform their world.* How important is choice? How does this relate to the Bible's view on free will? Have you experienced the power of choice in your own life?

_____

_____

_____

_____

_____

_____

_____

11. *There is no one like you, which means there is something you can do that no one else can do.* Does this mean we should compare ourselves to and compete with other people? What does our uniqueness mean in terms of human community? Should we celebrate our individuality? How do we celebrate our individuality by celebrating others?

_____

_____

_____

_____

_____

_____

_____

12. *Once you begin to understand your Perfect You and its structure—because truly getting to fully understand your Perfect You is a lifelong journey—you can walk in anticipation and freedom through life, rejoicing despite the circumstances.* Why do you think it is important to understand your Perfect You? How will this bring freedom, joy, and acceptance into your life?

---

13. *You, as the observer, keep updating your experience as new data from your experiences comes to light, shaping the way you approach the world.* Is your Perfect You unchanging? Is it always the same?

---

14. *The Perfect You will take you from missing the mark of being made in God's image to stepping into who you truly are.* How does the Perfect You help us to step into our role as image-bearers of God? How does it establish a sense of hope and purpose, as opposed to the hopelessness of pure naturalism with its focus on a short and ultimately purposeless life?

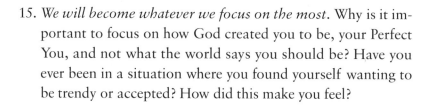

_____

_____

_____

_____

_____

_____

15. *We will become whatever we focus on the most.* Why is it important to focus on how God created you to be, your Perfect You, and not what the world says you should be? Have you ever been in a situation where you found yourself wanting to be trendy or accepted? How did this make you feel?

_____

_____

_____

_____

_____

_____

16. *Your Perfect You is the reflection of God—out of it springs your identity and your purpose as a steward of his creation and glory.* What is the definition of the Perfect You?

_____

_____

_____

_____

_____

_____

_____

17. *We must remember that success, in terms of shalom or biblical prosperity, is not defined by a collection of assets, an accumulation of power, or cash in the bank.* How do you define success in biblical terms? How do you understand success?

_____

_____

_____

_____

_____

_____

_____

_____

_____

DISCUSSION

In light of the information in this chapter, focusing on the hope that science gives us alongside Scripture, discuss the following verses:

1. **1 John 4:8 (ESV):** "Anyone who does not love does not know God, because God is love."

2. **2 Timothy 1:7 (AMP):** "For God did not give us a spirit of timidity or cowardice or fear, but [He has given us a spirit] of power and of love and of sound judgment and personal discipline [abilities that result in a calm, well-balanced mind and self-control]."

3. **Romans 12:2 (AMP):** "And do not be conformed to this world [any longer with its superficial values and customs], but be transformed and progressively changed [as you mature spiritually] by the renewing of your mind [focusing on godly values and ethical attitudes], so that you may prove [for yourselves] what the will of God is, that which is good and acceptable and perfect [in His plan and purpose for you]."

4. **Ephesians 4:16 (NLT):** "He makes the whole body fit together perfectly. As each part does its own special work, it helps the other parts grow, so that the whole body is healthy and growing and full of love."

5. **Psalm 139:14 (NLT):** "Thank you for making me so wonderfully complex! Your workmanship is marvelous—how well I know it."

Write your conclusions from the discussion of these Scriptures linked to the seventeen points above:

_____

_____

_____

_____

_____

_____

_____

_____

_____

_____

_____

_____

_____

_____

_____

_____

2

The Perfect You

Thinking, Feeling, Choosing

See pages 40–46 in *The Perfect You.*

1. *The Perfect You is a way of describing how we process and exhibit our uniqueness, or identity, through our ability to think, feel, and choose.* What are the two key components of the Perfect You? How do they work together?

_____

_____

_____

_____

_____

_____

_____

2. *If the brain is the physical substrate through which the Perfect You works, where our thoughts are stored, and from which we speak and act, then each human brain is uniquely attuned to each person.* Can you observe this uniqueness in your own life or in the lives of the people you know and love? Once again, it is helpful to think of a situation where you and someone you know experienced the same event yet perceived what was happening in very different ways.

_____

_____

_____

_____

_____

_____

_____

3. *Second Timothy 1:7 tells us we have love, power, and a sound mind.* How do you see this Scripture in terms of the science you are learning about in this book?

_____

_____

_____

_____

_____

_____

4. *Your Perfect You is exclusively yours; only you know what you are truly thinking, feeling, or choosing at any given moment.* How does the Perfect You relate to free will?

_____

_____

_____

_____

_____

_____

5. *Nothing determines your choices, or how you react to the circumstances of life, except you.* Do you feel that what you say, think, and do are solely determined by what happens to you? Think of a time when you found yourself in a difficult situation. Did you feel like you could choose how to react to what was going on? If you could go back in time, would you choose to react differently?

_____

_____

_____

_____

_____

_____

_____

6. *Every thought you think affects everyone else, and vice versa. Because everything was created in and through God, creation is entangled.* What is entanglement? If the world is entangled, how important is it for you to think, speak, and act with love? How does the scientific concept of entanglement relate to the biblical worldview?

_____

_____

_____

_____

_____

_____

7. *Relationships, of course, would not be relationships if we were all the same. Our differences shape and enhance our relationships.* Do you see the importance of differences in your relationships? Do you see these differences as complementary?

_____

_____

_____

_____

_____

_____

_____

8. *A loss of identity and purpose affects our ability to live our lives.* What is the World Health Organization's definition of mental health? How do you understand this definition in light of what the Bible says about mental well-being? Have you ever experienced a loss of identity and purpose? How did it affect you?

DISCUSSION

In light of the information in this chapter, focusing on the hope that science gives us alongside Scripture, discuss the following verses:

1. **John 1:1 (NIV):** "In the beginning was the Word, and the Word was with God, and the Word was God."

2. **1 Corinthians 2:16 (ESV):** "'For who has understood the mind of the Lord so as to instruct him?' But we have the mind of Christ."

3. **Acts 17:28 (ESV):** "For 'In him we live and move and have our being'; as even some of your own poets have said, 'For we are indeed his offspring.'"

4. **Mark 12:31 (NLT):** "The second is equally important: 'Love your neighbor as yourself.' No other commandment is greater than these."

5. **3 John 2 (NIV):** "Dear friend, I pray that you may enjoy good health and that all may go well with you, even as your soul is getting along well."

Write your conclusions from the discussion of these Scriptures linked to the eight points above:

_____

_____

_____

_____

_____

_____

_____

_____

_____

_____

_____

_____

_____

_____

_____

_____

_____

_____

_____

_____

_____

_____

_____

_____

3

Discovering the Potential of Our Blueprint for Identity

See pages 47–64 in *The Perfect You.*

1. *When we find out how we are human by understanding our uniqueness, we worship our glorious Creator!* What is meant by the word *worship*? How do you understand worship? What does worship have to do with identity and the Perfect You?

_____

_____

_____

_____

_____

_____

_____

2. *An attitude is a cluster of thoughts with emotional flavor, and every type of emotion has one of only two roots: love or fear.* What is the "love zone"? What does it mean to be "wired for love"? How does it relate to being made in the image of God? What is the human "default mode"? How do you understand "default mode" in relation to you and your experience of life?

_____

_____

_____

_____

_____

_____

3. *God blesses us by helping our brain detox, increasing our motivation and wisdom and helping us negotiate life more successfully when we operate in love.* How do you see this happening on a scientific level? Have you ever experienced this "love rush"?

_____

_____

_____

_____

_____

_____

_____

4. *When we are exposed to or think about something toxic, and there are thought clusters attached that include toxic emotions, they will set in motion a chemical cascade, launching our minds and bodies into toxic stress mode.* What happens to our bodies in this "toxic stress mode"? Have you ever experienced moments of toxic stress in your life? How did it make you feel? Did you feel like a different person in those moments? Did you lose your sense of "youness"? Have you ever felt like you were losing your sense of control?

_____

_____

_____

_____

_____

5. *We have incredible minds that are truly worth celebrating. We must also remember, however, that with the incredible power in our minds comes responsibility for how we use it: we cannot escape the consequences of our choices.* How does choice relate to the biblical worldview? The fact that we can choose how we react to life—in fear or in love—has huge implications for how we live our lives. How does this apply to you specifically?

_____

_____

_____

_____

_____

_____

43

6. *With the introduction of quantum physics theories in the 1920s, however, scientists realized that our intentional thinking, feeling, and choosing can make a difference in how the matter in our bodies behaves.* How was this view different to previously held views of humans? How does it compare to the biblical view of humanity? How is this applicable to your worldview? Does it challenge you, causing you to rethink how you see yourself?

_____

_____

_____

_____

_____

_____

7. *Normally incoming information goes through a certain route as it enters the brain, passing through structures as the information is being processed and creatively adding to our knowledge base. Neuroscientific research has been able to identify some of the important structures involved in this route.* What are some of these structures? How are they affected when we operate in love? And when we operate in fear? Why is this knowledge relevant to you? Does it make you realize how thinking has a causal effect? How? Why?

_____

_____

_____

_____

8. *The choice to overcome addictions is the most powerful and effective factor to overcoming addictive behavior.* How so? Have you found this in your life or in the lives of those you love? Do you see this in the stories of people who have overcome life-threatening addictions? Can you think of an example? Do you think that addictions are not just about the "big stuff" like cocaine and alcohol but include whatever is consuming you in a toxic direction? How does this relate to the idea of idolatry in the Bible? Examine your life—do you have some toxic addictions or idols?

_____

_____

_____

_____

_____

9. *God created us for relationship with him. Nothing else will satisfy this need to pray continuously and set up a constant internal dialogue with the Holy Spirit, so that we stay addicted to him, offering up our minds and bodies as a living sacrifice every day.* Do you find that if you do not focus on God and his Word, it is easy to become "addicted" to something else? What is that something else for you?

_____

_____

_____

_____

_____

10. *Every thought changes the brain chemistry, which impacts all 75–100 trillion cells of the body at quantum speeds.* What happens if these are positive thoughts? And what happens if these are negative thoughts? What really is "mental ill health"?

_____

_____

_____

_____

_____

_____

_____

11. *The more energy we give a toxic thought, the more it grows, and the more we feel consumed and trapped by it.* Have you experienced this in your life? What is happening in the human brain during this process?

_____

_____

_____

_____

_____

_____

_____

_____

12. *Science shows us that we need to practice using something or studying something at least seven times in repeated intervals over specific time frames before we are going to be able to use the information or perform the skill.* How long does this process of "renewing the mind" usually take? Is change immediate? Does it require discipline and hard work? Are you desperate enough to change and take time to find your Perfect You?

_____

_____

_____

_____

_____

_____

_____

13. *Each thought has its own chemical signature. The result is that your thinking quite literally becomes feeling with a resultant chemical reaction in your brain and body.* How does this relate to what the Bible says about thoughts? Have you experienced this in your own life? Have you ever felt "sick with stress"?

_____

_____

_____

_____

_____

_____

_____

14. *Epigenetics highlights our ability to respond to our environment, which includes everything from what we think to what we eat to what we generally understand by environmental exposure.* Why is this important in terms of controlling our thoughts and acting in the Perfect You?

_____

_____

_____

_____

_____

_____

_____

_____

15. *Our DNA is designed to react to the language of our thoughts and resultant words, as well as biological signals.* How so? Why is this important? What does this tell you about your intelligent and powerful mind?

_____

_____

_____

_____

_____

_____

_____

_____

16. *When we operate in love, our brains respond in the way they are designed to respond.* How does this work? Have you experienced this in your life? How does this relate to the mind-brain connection? What do you need to change to make sure you are using this mind-brain connection the way God designed it to be used? What is your role in this process?

DISCUSSION

In light of the information in this chapter, focusing on the hope that science gives us alongside Scripture, discuss the following verses:

1. **Psalm 148:7–12 (NIV):** "Praise the LORD from the earth, you great sea creatures and all ocean depths, lightning and hail, snow and clouds, stormy winds that do his bidding, you mountains and all hills, fruit trees and all cedars, wild animals and all cattle, small creatures and flying birds, kings of the earth and all nations, you princes and all rulers on earth, young men and women, old men and children."

2. **Deuteronomy 30:19 (NLT):** "Today I have given you the choice between life and death, between blessings and curses. Now I call on heaven and earth to witness the choice you make. Oh, that you would choose life, so that you and your descendants might live!"

3. **Galatians 5:22–23 (ESV):** "But the fruit of the Spirit is love, joy, peace, patience, kindness, goodness, faithfulness, gentleness, self-control."

4. **Luke 6:45 (ESV):** "The good person out of the good treasure of his heart produces good, and the evil person out of his evil treasure produces evil, for out of the abundance of the heart his mouth speaks."

5. **Ecclesiastes 7:29 (NIV):** "This only have I found: God created mankind upright, but they have gone in search of many
schemes."

Write your conclusions from the discussion of these Scriptures linked
to the sixteen points above:

_____

_____

_____

_____

_____

_____

_____

_____

_____

_____

_____

_____

_____

_____

_____

_____

_____

_____

4

The Philosophy of the Perfect You

See pages 67–77 in *The Perfect You.*

1. *A philosophy is a worldview, and it shapes our thinking.* What is meant by the term *worldview*? How do worldviews shape our thinking, choosing, and feeling?

_____

_____

_____

_____

_____

_____

_____

_____

2. *Since the advent of quantum physics and the search for the origins of the natural world of space and time, the face of science has changed. Matter has become difficult to define: atoms and electrons vs. possibilities, which aren't real until observed, equals physical vs. mind.* Even though this is a complicated concept, what does this tell you about the basic human need to search for the science of identity?

_____

_____

_____

_____

_____

_____

3. *Werner Heisenberg, a leader in the original formulation of quantum physics, said elementary particles like atoms and electrons are not "things" per se. These elementary particles form a world of pure possibilities.* How is this different from the way people usually understand solid matter and science in general? How do you understand the phrase "a world of pure possibilities"?

_____

_____

_____

_____

_____

_____

4. *Currently, there are two opposing worldviews in science: idealism (mind comes first) vs. materialism (brain comes first).* What are these two worldviews? How are they different? What are the implications of each worldview for thinking, feeling, and choosing? For you personally?

_____

_____

_____

_____

_____

_____

_____

5. *Idealism: The whole of reality, said the Nobel Prize laureate Eugene Wigner, is a construct of the mind.* How does this relate to the biblical worldview? What do you think consciousness is? Why is it so important to understand consciousness? How do consciousness and reality relate?

_____

_____

_____

_____

_____

_____

6. *What is real? Answer: The contents of consciousness—what is in your mind! The mind did not evolve out of the physical matter of the brain.* For followers of the Messiah, what are the challenges associated with a material worldview?

_____

_____

_____

_____

_____

_____

_____

_____

7. *In the beginning was the Word, or* logos *(see John 1:1–5). Logos is consciousness, which is intelligible, rational thought.* How does this passage relate to philosophical idealism? How do you relate this to what you believe?

_____

_____

_____

_____

_____

_____

_____

_____

_____

8. *God as consciousness was before the universe began. God's "mind" created everything and sustains everything (see Genesis 1–2; John 1; Acts 17:28). Quantum physics, with its examination of science beyond the traditional paradigms of space and time, points directly to the belief that the universe has a creative mind behind it (consciousness) and therefore a creative purpose. This understanding of consciousness supports the unique dignity of human personality found in the Bible: We are infinite minds made in the image of an infinite God.* How do you understand God as consciousness? How does this relate to the Bible? How does this way of seeing the world support human dignity?

_____

_____

_____

_____

_____

9. *The conscious world dominates, yet is intrinsic to, the physical world. This is the meeting of heaven and earth (see Matt. 6:9–13)!* How does this relate to idealism and quantum physics? How does this allow us to bring "heaven to earth"? How does Jesus bring heaven to earth? How does this help us stay in our Perfect You?

_____

_____

_____

_____

10. *Philosophical idealism is key to understanding your Perfect You. Mind produces matter. Your reality is constructed by your mind; that is, the collection of thoughts that are entirely yours as an individual, which are a reflection of the source of all reality: the mind of God (see 1 Cor. 2:16). As we uniquely perceive, so we create unique realities.* How so? Why is this so profoundly important to understand and to help you stay in your Perfect You? How do you understand the creative power of your mind?

_____

_____

_____

_____

_____

_____

11. *Materialism: A materialist worldview claims that the mind comes from matter.* What are the implications if mind comes from matter? Think about education, medicine—in fact, everything. Try to be specific: for example, in the way mental health is managed, how children are being taught at school, and so on.

_____

_____

_____

_____

_____

_____

12. *Materialism says that the physical or material aspect of think-ing is all that counts. In fact, it claims that the physical firing of the neurons produces the mind as a mere artifact, a mistake! Materialism claims you are what your brain does and that your unique thinking, feeling, and choosing are generated by the brain.* Why is this thinking so wrong? We have to start asking hard questions. Is being told you are a faulty machine, a bro-ken biological automaton, going to help bring peace, freedom, and healing? Are you extraneous to the equation because your brain is producing all your behaviors? Are you not able to have a decent relationship because a scan supposedly shows you have an ADHD brain or an fMRI supposedly shows you have schizophrenia (and, by the way, science shows this is incorrect— you cannot determine ADHD or schizophrenia from a brain scan, genetics, or bloodwork, because they are not diseases but rather symptoms of going through the sufferings of life)? Are you doomed to taking mind-altering meds for the rest of your life, often with disturbing side effects?

---

13. *Materialism also says everything that makes us human is simply an artifact of neurons firing and chemical reactions, proposing such ideas as identity theory (TFC = electrical impulses), determinism (cause/effect conditioning), and reductionism (this is your brain on . . .).* How is this back-to-front reasoning? Could this thinking confuse our identity? Our choices? How?

_____

_____

_____

_____

_____

_____

14. *Materialism has been essentially disproved, yet it still dominates many scientific fields.* How do you understand materialism? Can you think of some examples of this view in our world today? Was this the view you were taught in school? How does this contrast with the biblical worldview? How do you feel about the fact that materialism is disproved? What does this say for how you should respond to a diagnosis or a label put on you or a loved one?

_____

_____

_____

_____

_____

_____

15. *In many ways, materialism removes free will, hope, and responsibility. We become victims of biology, which opposes a biblical worldview that emphasizes choice and responsibility (Deut. 30:19). It medicalizes misery, emphasizing that our issues lie within our biology, not our social context or what we have gone through, including trauma, exploitation, or inept political structures. It often leads to incorrect scientific hypotheses and results.* Think of the ways that perhaps you have operated from a materialistic, deterministic worldview. Think of choices you have made regarding your health—what you eat, what you do, and how you think about things on a day-to-day basis. What worldview is really influencing you? Take the time to think about the motives and ideas that shape your thinking, feeling, and choosing.

16. *Nobel Prize laureate John Eccles said that "the essential feature of dualist interactionism is that the mind and brain are independent entities . . . and that they interact by quantum physics." Interactive-dualism provokes a real exploration of the deepest things of science, which point back to God and taking responsibility for what we think, feel, and choose. Each of us think, feel, and choose with our minds. Neuroscience and classical physics only describe the physical response of the brain to the mind-in-action, the mind being the first cause. Interactive-dualism is a philosophical framework for understanding the nonphysical mind. As we uniquely perceive, so we create unique realities.* How is interactive-dualism different from materialism? How does this worldview relate to the Bible? How does it show the huge responsibility we have in developing our Perfect You within ourselves in order not to abuse the gift of free will? How does this tie into a Christlike mindset? How can interactive-dualism help us understand how to create realities that are in alignment with God's plan to bring heaven to earth?

---

17. *As we uniquely perceive, so we create unique realities. We need to develop the same mindset as Christ so that we can create realities that are in alignment with God's plan to bring heaven to earth.* How is this different from materialism? How does this relate to idealism and the Bible?

_____

_____

_____

_____

_____

_____

_____

_____

18. *Each of us think, feel, and choose with our minds. Neuroscience and classical physics only describe the physical response of the brain to the mind-in-action, the mind being the first cause.* What does this mean in terms of identity in your life?

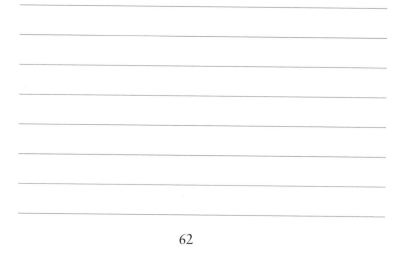

19. *The brain is the substrate through which the mind works—it reflects the action of the mind. The mind controls the brain; the brain does not control the mind.* Explain this in your own words, and also explain what this means for you and your blueprint for identity.

_____

_____

_____

_____

_____

_____

20. *Quantum physics, with its examination of science beyond the traditional paradigms of space and time, points directly to the belief that the universe has a creative mind behind it (consciousness), and therefore a creative purpose.* How does this make you feel in terms of hope and control and your future?

_____

_____

_____

_____

_____

_____

_____

21. *This understanding of consciousness supports the unique dignity of human personality found in the Bible: we are infinite minds made in the image of an infinite God.* What are the effects this statement has on you? How is this going to change how you see yourself?

_____

_____

_____

_____

_____

_____

_____

_____

_____

_____

DISCUSSION

In light of the information in this chapter, focusing on the hope that science gives us alongside Scripture, discuss the following verses:

1. **1 Corinthians 2:16** (**NLT**): "But we understand these things, for we have the mind of Christ."
2. **John 1:4–5** (**NLT**): "The Word gave life to everything that was created, and his life brought light to everyone. The light shines in the darkness, and the darkness can never extinguish it."
3. **1 Thessalonians 5:23** (**NIV**): "May God himself, the God of peace, sanctify you through and through. May your whole spirit, soul and body be kept blameless at the coming of our Lord Jesus Christ."
4. **Matthew 22:37** (**NIV**): "Jesus replied: 'Love the Lord your God with all your heart and with all your soul and with all your mind.'"
5. **Jeremiah 4:23** (**ESV**): "I looked on the earth, and behold, it was without form and void; and to the heavens, and they had no light."

Write your conclusions from the discussion of these Scriptures linked to the twenty-one points above:

_____

_____

5

The Science of the Perfect You

> See pages 78–106 in *The Perfect You.*

1. *The Perfect You—the unique way we think, feel, and choose—is the driving force behind our natural, wired-for-love design. It is at the core of our being, expressed through how we think, feel, and choose—what we say and do.* Describe yourself in a few lines based on this definition.

_____

_____

_____

_____

_____

_____

THE PERFECT YOU WORKBOOK

2. *The Perfect You is a particular reflection of God in this world, our unique way of worshiping him by thinking, feeling, and choosing well.* What is meant by this statement? What does this mean: "It is a byproduct of living according to our truth value"? What are the implications of the Perfect You if it has been designed by God to reflect his glory to the world?

_____

_____

_____

_____

_____

_____

3. *The Perfect You is a filter that designates how we as individuals process—think, feel, and choose—information.* Think of an example that demonstrates this difference; for example, compare you and someone else having a discussion about something.

_____

_____

_____

_____

_____

_____

_____

4. *When people ask me why they should know about their Perfect You, my answer is simple: knowing your Perfect You will unlock you and set you free to be you, a particular reflection of the Creator, which fulfills your sense of purpose, increasing your intelligence and your joy in the process.* What does this mean to you? How do you think understanding the science and theory behind the Perfect You is going to help you achieve this goal? Can you see science as another analogy for understanding the transcendence of God? How so?

_____

_____

_____

_____

5. *Trauma and sin can interrupt the Perfect You design: people seek love in other directions in an attempt to recapture the feeling of being truly themselves by bringing some level of order in their minds and bodies. Yet there is always hope.* How do you process reality? What happens if your filter is toxic? How are toxic patterns created? What is this chaos? Have you experienced this in your life? How does it manifest for you specifically? Can you link the triggers to your reactions and notice a pattern?

_____

_____

_____

_____

THE PERFECT YOU WORKBOOK

6. *The Perfect You is still stronger than negative thought patterns, and this is why I am encouraging you to get a grip on the science of the Perfect You. It will take you beyond just nice-to-know "I am a child of the King" phrases to the depths of what reflecting the image of our glorious and eternal King really means.* What have you learned from the science of thought about your ability to control toxic thought patterns? How do you think understanding the science and theory behind the Perfect You is going to help you achieve this goal?

_____

_____

_____

_____

_____

7. *The Perfect You design has a structure that can be explained using the Geodesic Information Processing Model I developed nearly thirty years ago.* What are the components of this model? Do they work together or separately? What controls these components? What is active self-regulation? What is metacognitive action? Are you just one module, or a mix? I know this is quite technical, but have a go at understanding and explaining anyway! Stretching your mind is so good for brain health!

_____

_____

_____

_____

_____

8. *Functioning in the Perfect You means you will say and do the best for that situation, and the geodesic model explains how this works.* Why is this important to understanding your whole, complex Perfect You? Dig deep and be very introspective as you answer this—you will be amazed at what you know when you really challenge yourself to think things through to another level!

_____

_____

_____

_____

_____

9. *There are seven metacognitive modules: interpersonal, intrapersonal, linguistic, logical/mathematical, kinesthetic, musical, and visual/spatial. The seven metacognitive modules of my geodesic model differ from the seven intelligences of Howard Gardner's "multiple intelligences" theory.* How are they different from other intelligence tests? Why is the Perfect You less restrictive and static? Why is this important to operating in the Perfect You?

_____

_____

_____

_____

_____

71

PLEASE NOTE: This question 10 is separate points (10/11/12) on the DVD slideshow for teaching purposes, which are combined together here to answer as one question.

10. *The metacognitive modules are divided into four processing systems: read, speak, listen, and write. Each processing system is divided into three metacognitive domains—what, how, and when/why. The processing systems and metacognitive domains in the geodesic model reflect the idea that human beings are so constituted as to be sensitive to certain information in their own unique way. Embracing your Perfect You will maximize the selection and integration of functions into the most efficient processing systems to operationalize the cognitive acts, result-ing in optimal performance. This means you will say and do the best for that situation.* Think of a time you felt amazing, or said something that lifted someone's spirits, or did well in a test or exam or situation, or were very creative and got excited about it. How did that feel? Re-create the situation and analyze its what, how, and when/why. In this exercise, you are actually examining the elements of your nonconscious mind and the structure of your specific memories.

PLEASE NOTE: This is 13 on the slideshow because of the combined questions above.

11. *In order to be able to read that novel or give that speech, you need to activate or operationalize the processing system. This is called dynamic self-regulation, a very powerful driving force of your nonconscious mind-in-action and very specific to your Perfect You.* What is dynamic self-regulation? How does it work? How is it different from active self-regulation?

_____

_____

_____

_____

_____

PLEASE NOTE: This is 14 on the slideshow because of the combined questions above.

12. *Active self-regulation is conscious thinking and also where choices happen, almost like a second level of decision-making. The particular way you build and store memories is based on your specific perception and interpretation, which is exclusive to you.* How so? Have you seen this in your own life?

_____

_____

_____

_____

THE PERFECT YOU WORKBOOK

PLEASE NOTE: This question 13 is separate points (15/16/17) on the DVD slideshow for teaching purposes, which are combined together here to answer as one question.

13. *Metacognitive action is when dynamic and active self-regulation interact, which happens through deliberate, intentional thinking. This is Perfect You thinking, and it is optimized when we involve the Holy Spirit. Mindful, intentional, and deliberate active self-regulation will activate interaction between active and dynamic self-regulation, the result of which is thinking deeply.* What is this deep thinking called? What happens when we think deeply in a deliberate way? What is metacognitive action? Why is this so important? Have you noticed I make this comment repeatedly through the book, DVD, and this workbook? Why?

_____

_____

_____

_____

_____

_____

_____

_____

_____

_____

_____

_____

_____

PLEASE NOTE: This is 18 on the slideshow because of the combined questions above.

14. *Scientists see traces of this nonconscious dynamic self-regulation activity in what is called the "readiness potential."* What is the readiness potential? Can you see the link between a readiness potential that is based on Perfect You habits versus toxic habits? Think about the biblical story of the woman with the issue of blood and the kinds of habits she had built into her nonconscious mind that formed the action potential that helped her recognize the "goodness" in Jesus as the source of her miracle. Think about examples in your own life and write them down.

_____

_____

_____

_____

_____

_____

_____

_____

_____

_____

_____

_____

_____

_____

PLEASE NOTE: This is 19 and 20 on the slideshow on the DVD.

15. *Metacognitive action: self-regulation, self-evaluation, capturing thoughts, renewing mindsets. The more the seven metacognitive modules interact, the more that deep thinking (called metacognitive action) kicks in and the wiser we become.* What is wisdom? How does the Holy Spirit help us grow in wisdom? How is it scientifically linked to deep thinking?

_____

_____

_____

_____

_____

_____

_____

_____

_____

_____

_____

_____

_____

_____

PLEASE NOTE: This question 16 is separate points 21/22/23/24 on the DVD slideshow for teaching purposes, which are combined together here.

16. *The more the seven metacognitive modules interact, the more that deep thinking kicks in and the wiser we become. All seven metacognitive modules work together in a simultaneous, entangled fashion, and in unique ways for each of us. This uniqueness represents individualistic thinking, feeling, and choosing. Strength in the sum of the parts is the fundamental principle of this modular perspective.* What does this mean to you and why is it so important to understand? There is a spiritual link here—what is it?

PLEASE NOTE: This is 25 on the slideshow because of the combined questions above.

17. *When you operate in your Perfect You, you are learning well.* What is learning? How is it related to worldview? How do you learn well in the Perfect You?

_____

_____

_____

_____

_____

PLEASE NOTE: The next three questions are not on the DVD but they are important, so I have included them here for you to answer. The answers are in the book.

18. *The brain has a quantum nature, shown by quantum physics calculations and quantum neurobiology, that cannot be adequately explained by classical physics.* How is quantum physics related to consciousness, the mind, and choice? How does this help us develop a deeper insight into the transcendent nature of God?

_____

_____

_____

_____

_____

19. *As the stimuli of the events of life enter into your brain through your five senses, your unique structurally and spiritually designed Perfect You filters the information, and this specific activity fires up your brain. No one knows what you are going to choose except you. There is an infinite number of probabilities you can choose from—good and bad, which in quantum theory is spoken of in terms of Erwin Schrödinger's probability wave. Schrödinger's equation predicts probability—but it is just a prediction, so there is always a degree of uncertainty as to the outcome. This scientific explanation has a powerful impact on how you choose.* How do you view choices and consequences now that you have studied this section? How do you see them in light of faith: for example, in reference to Hebrews 11:1?

_____

_____

_____

_____

_____

_____

_____

_____

_____

_____

_____

_____

20. *We are made to interact with each other and help each other even when we are going through hard times. Quantum mechanics, with its emphasis on the entangled nature of consciousness and the physical world, is about us in the world, not the world or us. "Us in the world" becomes key to the release of the Perfect You.* How does entanglement relate to the biblical worldview? How does it relate to you and your relationships? How does it relate to forgiveness?

DISCUSSION

In light of the information in this chapter, focusing on the hope that science gives us alongside Scripture, discuss the following verses:

1. **Philippians 4:8 (NLT):** "Fix your thoughts on what is true, and honorable, and right, and pure, and lovely, and admirable. Think about things that are excellent and worthy of praise."

2. **James 1:21 (NIV):** "Therefore, get rid of all moral filth and the evil that is so prevalent and humbly accept the word planted in you, which can save you."

3. **Matthew 13:1–9 (ESV):** "That same day Jesus went out of the house and sat beside the sea. And great crowds gathered about him, so that he got into a boat and sat down. And the whole crowd stood on the beach. And he told them many things in parables, saying: 'A sower went out to sow. And as he sowed, some seeds fell along the path, and the birds came and devoured them. Other seeds fell on rocky ground, where they did not have much soil, and immediately they sprang up, since they had no depth of soil, but when the sun rose they were scorched. And since they had no root, they withered away. Other seeds fell among thorns, and the thorns grew up and choked them. Other seeds fell on good soil and produced grain, some a hundredfold, some sixty, some thirty. He who has ears, let him hear.'"

4. **Ephesians 4:16 (NLT):** "He makes the whole body fit together perfectly. As each part does its own special work, it helps the other parts grow, so that the whole body is healthy and growing and full of love."

5. **Romans 8:19–21 (ESV):** "For the creation waits with eager longing for the revealing of the sons of God. For the creation was subjected to futility, not willingly, but because of him who subjected it, in hope that the creation itself will be set free from its bondage to corruption and obtain the freedom of the glory of the children of God."

Write your conclusions from the discussion of these Scriptures linked to the twenty points above:

_____

_____

_____

_____

_____

_____

_____

_____

_____

_____

_____

_____

6 AND 7

Profiling the Perfect You

The Unique Qualitative (UQ) Assessment Tool

and

The Perfect You Checklist

See pages 109–238 in *The Perfect You.*

You are now ready to do the *Unique Qualitative (UQ) Assess-ment* profile. Follow the instructions in the book and fill it in as intensively as you can. This profile is an organic process that is ongoing and can be repeated at least once a year. The UQ is the tool that will help you unlock your Perfect You and begin to access your true nature. It is a way of *intentionally* attempting to understand *how* we think, feel, and choose, and how each individual brain is organized to reflect a particular way of thinking, feeling, and choosing.

The UQ is *not*:

1. an IQ test
2. a personality test
3. an EQ or SQ
4. 1, 2, 3 = derivatives of materialism that put you in a box, label you, and limit your future to the snapshot of the now

The UQ *does*:

1. go beyond IQ, EQ, SQ, and personality tests
2. focus on individuality and uniqueness
3. account for limitless potential and unpredictability

The Greek philosopher Aristotle explained it this way: we each have *potentia*, which are "objective tendencies" (to use Heisenberg's quantum physics description) that enable us to express ourselves and are the result of our choices. No one knows what you are going to choose or what your "actuality" is going to be (to use another Aristotelian concept). These potentia are unlimited and immeasurable; only you and God know them, until you choose to make a potential into an actual choice that impacts you and your world. The UQ profile recognizes and honors the Aristotelian potentia in you.

As discussed under the science of the Perfect You, a metacognitive module is a cluster of intellectual abilities that form the raw material of thought and make up the structure of the nonconscious mind. These modules influence the thinking process: each module produces a specific type of thought based on its nature. There are seven types and, hence, seven sections to the UQ assessment. Processing of information (thinking, feeling, and choosing) is the result of how these modules interact and are used. You have your own unique thought-processing pattern, which is comprised of how you use the content of each module and how your modules interact.

The questions are designed to help you unlock and understand how *you* use these modules. We all do everything you see in the questions below, just differently. In fact, these modules are all essential processing skills that make up your UQ profile, so do not make the mistake of focusing on one and thinking you are, for example, just a visual/spatial learner or a logical/mathematical learner. This is a reductionist mistake that comes from years of doing IQ, EQ, SQ, and other kinds of personality tests. It is imperative to grasp that these elements of your Perfect You are the raw computational capacities that combine together to reflect you. *The accurate reflection of your "youness" is in the sum of the parts—not the parts alone!*

As you move through this UQ assessment, you will become consciously aware of how you *specifically* use these raw computational capacities. These are probing questions that are designed to help you understand you, so dig and think deeply before answering each one. The more seriously you answer them, the more you will understand yourself.

There is no one correct answer. Every answer is correct, regardless of whether yes or no is part of your answer. But a yes or no alone is not enough—you must write as much as you can, in as fully descriptive sentences as possible. Treat this as the process of asking, answering, and discussing as you work through the questions in a deliberate, intentional, and self-regulatory way.

❖

Once you have done the profile, go to chapter 7 and study, do, and memorize the *Perfect You checklist* and the *thanksgiving, praise, and worship exercise.* This checklist is an amazing tool to help you be constantly self-evaluative and self-reflective.

I strongly recommend you do all this before going on to the next section—you will get a lot more out of this next section if you follow the order I am suggesting.

8

The Discomfort Zones

See pages 241–61 in *The Perfect You.*

1. *You were created with intention, purpose, and greatness. You were designed to live in your Perfect You.* After completing the UQ assessment, how has your perception of your identity changed? How do you understand being made "in the image of God"?

_____

_____

_____

_____

_____

_____

_____

_____

2. *The UQ assessment you completed has a threefold purpose: to help you understand how you uniquely think, feel, and choose; to increase your ability to mindfully and deliberately self-regulate—thinking, feeling, and choosing to keep in alignment with the Holy Spirit; and to help you understand how you think when you are operating in your Perfect You so that you can recognize when you are operating outside of it.* How does the UQ profile do this?

3. *We have a mind, we live in a body, and we are a spirit.* How do these three parts work together?

4. *Discomfort zones are zones in our spirits, minds, and bodies that alert us to when we are stepping out of our Perfect You. They sound the "alarm" in our consciousness when we step out of the love zone and into the damaging fear zone.* What are the discomfort zones or "warning signals" in your life?

_____

_____

_____

_____

_____

_____

_____

5. *Discomfort zones are gracious "prompts" from God to keep us in his love zone by increasing our awareness of our thoughts, feelings, and choices so we can self-regulate them. There are four main discomfort zone levels that we sequence through.* What are these levels? What is the purpose of a discomfort zone?

_____

_____

_____

_____

_____

_____

6. *The spiritual element of the discomfort zones occurs when the opposites of the fruit of the Spirit (Gal. 5:22–23) activate in our minds.* What happens on the spiritual level of each of the discomfort zones? What two purposes do the spiritual alarms at each level tell you? Have you experienced this in your life? If so, how?

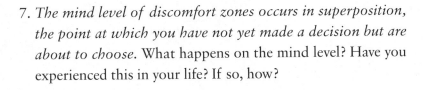

7. *The mind level of discomfort zones occurs in superposition, the point at which you have not yet made a decision but are about to choose.* What happens on the mind level? Have you experienced this in your life? If so, how?

8. *The body level of discomfort zones directly reflects the spirit and mind.* What happens on the body level? Have you experienced this in your life? If so, how?

_____

_____

_____

_____

_____

9. *If we can train ourselves to identify and use the four discomfort zones, we are well on the way to being freed from the chains of toxicity and the fear attitudes they produce and stepping into our Perfect You. Study the detailed explanations of the sequence of the discomfort zones and how the spirit, mind, and body alarms work in each on pages 241–61 in* The Perfect You. Once you have done this and understand them fully, think about how to train yourself to identify your discomfort zones. How would you do this as a lifestyle habit? Can you think of a way you can make this a daily activity?

_____

_____

_____

_____

_____

9 AND 10

The Perfect You Chart

and

Perfect You Metacognitive Module Exercises

See pages 262–80 in *The Perfect You.*

In chapter 9 you will find a great chart that is a summary of all the concepts in the book to help you remember them!

- The chart tracks the process from the point at which you focus on the information to the point at which choices are being made.
- You will see four columns that you read from left to right.
- Column 1 deals with the incoming signals of the events and circumstances of life.
- Column 2 tracks the philosophy and science of this.
- Column 3 provides examples.

- Column 4 shows how to use the discomfort zones to stay in your Perfect You.

In chapter 10, there are exercises to help you:

- Become aware of how you think in your Perfect You state.
- Improve how you use the seven metacognitive modules, as well as to increase their interaction. (Remember, the strength of your Perfect You is in the sum of the parts operating as a whole system. You cannot single out one metacognitive module and describe it as your "strength.")
- Recognize when you step out of your Perfect You.
- Develop your intellect.

How to Use the Perfect You Exercises

When it comes to using the Perfect You exercises, I recommend working through them in the sequence suggested in chapter 10 of the book, spending as many days on each as you feel necessary. Use the Perfect You checklist (see pages 236–37) *every day* and, in addition, carve out minutes in your day to work on these exercises. My recommendation is to do one per day or one per week—whatever works best for you—until you have done them all, and then repeat them. These are not exercises to do once and then forget about; they are actually deliberate, lasting changes you are going to be making to develop and stay in your Perfect You. They are part of a lifestyle of continual growth.

So, on a practical level, you could read through an exercise first thing in the morning, type it into your smartphone or write it on a card, and practice it through the day. If you are already doing my twenty-one-day brain detox (see www.21daybraindetox.com and my book *Switch On Your Brain*), you can use these exercises as part of your *active reaches*.

Conclusion

Congratulations! You have almost completed *The Perfect You Workbook*. You have begun the process of finding your blueprint for identity, but remember this is a lifetime task. It is important to remember that neither the *Perfect You* nor this workbook is an instant, quick-fix solution that will tell you who you are and what you should do.

As we experience everyday life, the "talk" between the conscious and nonconscious mind discussed in *The Perfect You* develops, shaping the way we think, feel, and choose. The more we become aware of this talk, the more we understand and shape who we are through the gift of the freedom of choice, and the more we are able to reflect the image of God into the world.

The Perfect You book, workbook, and DVD are tools that will empower you to discover your unique way of thinking, feeling, and choosing—your blueprint for identity. They can be used multiple times, since there is no expiration date on your "youness." Regardless of where you are in your life, change is possible.

You can be the divine image–bearing person you were created to be—all you have to do is choose to start living out of your brilliant blueprint for identity!

The Perfect You Reading List

Nick Collins, "IQ Tests 'Do Not Reflect Intelligence,'" *The Telegraph*, December 19, 2012, http://www.telegraph.co.uk/news/science/science-news/9755929/IQ-tests-do-not-reflect-intelligence.html.

Haverford College, "IQ Tests Are Biased Against Certain Groups," *The Psychology Of*, accessed October 24, 2017, https://sites.google.com/a/haverford.edu/the-psychology-of/contact/iq-tests-are-biased-against-certain-groups.

Christian Jarrett, PhD, "Why the Left-Brain Right-Brain Myth Will Probably Never Die," *Psychology Today*, June 27, 2012, https://www.psychologytoday.com/blog/brain-myths/201206/why-the-left-brain-right-brain-myth-will-probably-never-die.

"The Left Brain Vs. Right Brain Myth—Elizabeth Waters," *Ted-Ed*, accessed October 24, 2017, https://ed.ted.com/lessons/the-left-brain-vs-right-brain-myth-elizabeth-waters.

J. Richard Middleton, "The Role of Human Beings in the Cosmic Temple: The Intersection of Worldviews in Psalms 8 and 104," *Canadian Theological Review* vol. 2, no. 1 (2013), https://jrichardmiddleton.files.wordpress.com/2014/02/middleton-role-of-human-beings-in-the-cosmic-temple-ctr-2013-v2-1.pdf.

J. Richard Middleton, "A New Heaven and a New Earth: The Case for a Holistic Reading of the Biblical Story of Redemption," *Journal for Christian Theological Research* vol. 11 (2006): 73–97, https://jrichardmiddleton.files.wordpress.com/2013/10/middleton-a-new-heaven-and-a-new-earth-essay.pdf.

ALSO AVAILABLE FROM
DR. CAROLINE LEAF

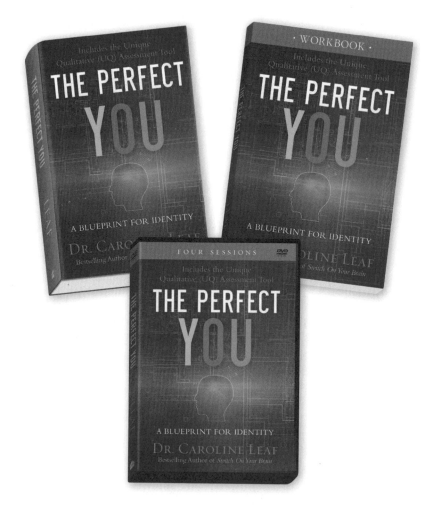

Science and Scripture show you're a unique, brilliantly designed, and intelligent individual who fills a role no one else can. So the more Perfect You you become, the more fulfilling and impactful your life will be. In this book, Dr. Caroline Leaf tackles this concept from theological, philosophical, and scientific angles, challenging you to think deeply about your identity and enabling you to apply these insights to your daily life.

BakerBooks
a division of Baker Publishing Group
www.BakerBooks.com

Available wherever books and ebooks are sold.